THE SOUTH DEVON RAILWAY

50 YEARS OF HERITAGE OPERATION

Bernard Warr

AMBERLEY

First published 2019

Amberley Publishing
The Hill, Stroud
Gloucestershire, GL5 4EP

www.amberley-books.com

ISBN 978 1 4456 8571 7 (print)
ISBN 978 1 4456 8572 4 (ebook)

British Library Cataloguing in Publication Data.
A catalogue record for this book is available from
the British Library.

Origination by Amberley Publishing.
Printed in the UK.

Introduction

Casting my mind back fifty-three years I can vividly remember a warm summer's day back in 1966 and riding down a leafy Devon road in a friend's car. We came upon the town of Buckfastleigh and paused at the gated approach road to the long-closed railway station. The surprise of seeing dark green engines and chocolate and cream coaches slumbering in the warm afternoon sunshine can be imagined! My friend Nigel, whose car it was, was entranced. We got out to have a closer look.

The gate was padlocked but a notice proclaimed that this was the Dart Valley Railway. A smaller typewritten notice advised that the company intended to reopen the Totnes to Ashburton branch line as a tourist attraction and was looking for volunteers to help bring it back to life. Anyone interested in helping should write to Mr R. D. N. Salisbury, Hon. Sec. of the supporting Dart Valley Railway Association. My interest was awakened and I made a note of the contact address. Within a few days I became the ninety-seventh member.

I learnt that restoration working parties were held every Sunday and I decided to join in. Another Sunday two weeks later found me alighting from the maroon and cream Devon General bus from Exeter and entering the Buckfastleigh station yard. I had been warned to dress in old clothes as the work tended to be 'physical' and dirty!

On arrival at the station I found a small gang of people waiting to start work, who were in the charge of a grey-haired old gentleman whose accent had a rich Devon burr. He introduced himself as Ashley Burgess and explained that he was the recently retired British Railways Permanent Way Inspector from Totnes. He had been responsible for maintaining the branch when British Railways had been in charge and he was now a volunteer, keen to help get the trains running.

He explained that the task for the day was to get the points back in working order. It seemed they had lain derelict for four years since the last goods train had run and the moist Devon air had caused the rods and cranks to rust up solid. When the various locomotives and carriages had been moved up the branch from Totnes, the point rodding had been disconnected and the points moved with a crowbar (which I now learnt was called a 'slewing-bar' in railway parlance), and then 'clamped' with a big, lockable 'G' clamp.

We set to work with a will, starting from the signal box and working outwards. The technique I learnt was to soak the crank pivot in a light oil, disconnect the rodding from each end of the crank and then gently tap the crank arms alternately with a sledgehammer (being careful not to snap off the brittle cast-iron crank arm). If this failed to produce a result, then a propane torch was produced and the pivot gently heated. More gentle tapping was usually enough to allow the crank to be moved and released from its pivot. It was then a simple matter of cleaning and greasing the components, reassembling them and moving on to the next crank.

At some point in the day we must have broken off for lunch but Ashley was a hard taskmaster and didn't let us sit around for long! At the end of that first day I suppose we must have dealt with about six or seven cranks and got thoroughly dirty in the process. There were no washing facilities then, so I had to travel back on the Exeter bus as I was. Despite this I felt an extreme sense of having done something useful; something that would help bring this little railway back to life. I resolved to come again the next week.

I went back to the Dart Valley Railway many times in that far-off summer of 1966. The Permanent Way gang that I seemed to have joined attended to all sorts of problems on and about the railway. We cut back the rampant undergrowth; we mended fences; we oiled fishplates; we hammered keys back in; we packed joints; we freed more point rods and cranks; and we cut back the undergrowth again. Prominent among the members of the gang was Barry Cogar, who was to become a life-long friend (and General Manager and Director of the company).

Sadly, my developing career took me away from Devon but despite this I have remained an ardent supporter of the line and I still carry membership card 97, although my membership of the Dart Valley Railway Association has become membership of the South Devon Railway Association.

The line has a long history. Built as a broad gauge line by the Buckfastleigh, Totnes & South Devon Railway, it opened through to Ashburton on 1 May 1872 and was operated from the start by the SDR (which became part of the GWR in 1876). Along with other GWR lines in the South West it was converted to standard gauge in 1892. The line is reputed to have never made a profit despite having regular freight traffic of cattle, wool and cider going out with coal and agricultural machinery coming in.

With the nationalisation of the railways in 1948 it became part of the Western Region of British Railways, but even then the growth of the motor vehicle had made serious inroads into the core traffic. The passenger service was discontinued from 3 November 1958 and freight traffic was only able to continue until 7 September 1962. As the following photographs will show, nature started to take over the trackbed, with saplings and weeds growing right across it.

However, it seemed as though the last engine had hardly had time to drop its fire before the local press revealed that a group of businessmen, including Patrick Whitehouse and Pat Garland (both of BBC *Railway Roundabout* fame) and local businessmen Bob Saunders, Rob Woodman and others, was planning to reopen the line as a steam-operated branch line. Their business plan was to launch and operate a profitable summer season tourist railway, focused on the many visitors who choose to holiday in South Devon.

Forming the Dart Valley Light Railway Company Ltd, it took ownership of the branch line in October 1965 and on 2 October of that year the first rolling stock arrived: GWR locomotives Nos 4555 and 3205 and four BR(W) auto trailers.

In 1966 a Light Railway Order was granted to permit operation; however, the Ministry of Transport insisted that the railway assist in improvements to the A38 road and it was not until 1969 that an agreement was made to operate from Totnes to Buckfastleigh, with the section beyond to Ashburton in abeyance and subject to further negotiations.

The first passenger trains ran on the Dart Valley Railway on 5 April 1969, hauled by GWR Pannier tank locomotive No. 6412. The official opening, undertaken by no less than Dr Beeching, followed on 21 May 1969. Sadly, the last 2 miles of the line to Ashburton were never operated and in 1971, a year short of the line's centenary, the line was severed to make way for the widening of the A38 road and the beautiful Brunel station at Ashburton lost its trains.

In 1971, the company was presented the chance to purchase the GWR Kingswear Branch, running from Paignton to Kingswear, from BR. To complete the purchase a public limited company (plc) was created and a share offer made. The flotation was successful and, in 1972, the original preservation company became the Dart Valley Railway Company plc. The purchase price of the railway was £250,000 and a further £25,000 was paid for signalling alterations at Paignton. Most of this was recouped from the sale of surplus land, mainly at Goodrington, which was subsequently developed as flats, and at Kingswear, which became a marina.

In 1989, the Dart Valley Railway plc announced that the Buckfastleigh–Totnes line was uneconomical, stating that they had decided to either find another operator or close it. The volunteers who had been involved with operating the line realised this was now their chance to form a company to take over the railway and run it as a registered charity. Fortunately, there was a registered charity already based on the line, Dumbleton Hall Locomotive Ltd, which was busy restoring GWR No. 4920 *Dumbleton Hall*. Its Articles of Association, far-sightedly, allowed it to run a railway, so it began to negotiate terms for a lease of the Buckfastleigh line. These were successful and the new company commenced operations on 1 January 1991. The charity was renamed the South Devon Railway Trust and the railway was renamed the South Devon Railway – the name of the first company to run trains over the line. The volunteer supporting body was similarly renamed the South Devon Railway Association. The first train under SDR operation ran on 29 March 1991 with BR(W) Pannier tank locomotive No. 1638 and a rake of former BR coaches, all hired from the Dart Valley company.

The use of DVR locos and stock could only ever be a temporary measure as the traffic demands of the Paignton to Kingswear line necessitated a goodly number of carriages and locos. The SDRA had a substantial financial stake in Small Prairie No. 4588, having raised the funds to buy it from Barry Scrapyard in the first place. Negotiation with the DVR plc resulted in the ownership of this loco passing to the DVR in exchange for 14xx 0-4-2T No. 1420 and two auto trailers. The Weymouth Dock tank, No. 1369, was also acquired by the SDR. Coaching stock was a problem in the early years but several coaches were acquired from a variety of sources, including the vehicles that were long-term Newton Abbot residents outside David & Charles Publishers. Supporters helped with locomotives and two ex-WD Austerity saddle tanks, *Errol Lonsdale* and *Sapper,* were the mainstays of the fleet at one stage.

Probably the most significant early development for the new operator was to obtain grant funding to construct a pedestrian footbridge across the River Dart at Totnes.

This was opened in 1993 and immediately enhanced the status of Totnes Littlehempston station from a run-round loop and platform in a field to a proper station with access to and from Totnes main line railway station and town centre.

In 2000, the SDR started negotiations to purchase the freehold of the line from the DVR for £1.15 million, the money being raised through a share issue, loans, donations and revenue. In 2002, the DVR granted the SDR a 199 lease on condition of a new Transport & Works Order (TWO) being granted to the SDR, which would allow the grant of the final transfer of the freehold title from the DVR to the SDR for the payment of a nominal £1.

In 2004, with the help of the Heritage Lottery Fund, the line's major crossing of the River Dart, Nursey Pool Bridge, was reconstructed to modern loading standards, effectively removing the limitation on the size of locomotives that could pass over the line.

In 2007, the line carried over 100,000 passengers for the first time and was named Heritage Railway of the Year. In 2009 the SDR celebrated the 40th anniversary of the line's reopening.

On 8 February 2010, the final step of the protracted TWO process was completed: the SDR paid the nominal £1 and became masters of their own destiny!

In the twenty-eight years since the charitable trust took over, the line has been expanded enormously, building a loop at Staverton to enable two-train running, completing the station buildings at Totnes, expanding facilities at Buckfastleigh, carrying out major civil engineering works on the line, undertaking major resignalling works (including the re-erection of two historic GWR signal boxes), establishing a flourishing engineering business and, importantly, attracting more and more visitors to come and visit.

2019 will see another milepost reached and is likely to be a year of celebration for the South Devon Railway. On 5 April 2019, it will be fifty years since the first train ran in the heritage era. We must look forward to the next fifty years!

Assembling this collection of images has been something of a 'labour of love' and has brought back many happy memories. I have been fortunate to be able to call on other photographers to make up for the shortfall in my own collection and I am indebted to Bernard Mills for allowing me to use his comprehensive collection of images so freely. I must also thank my brother Stuart Warr for his contribution and Connor Stait at Amberley Publishing for his continued encouragement and support.

Bernard Warr
Market Rasen, Lincolnshire
January 2019

In the period after the total closure of the branch in 1962, vegetation growth was unchecked. This is a view of Staverton taken from the Ashburton end in October 1964. (The late Colin L. Caddy/BW Collection)

With the last train having run in 1962 it didn't take long for nature to reassert itself. This was how the approach to Ashburton station looked when the infant Dart Valley Railway got access to the line in June 1965. (Bernard Mills)

By April 1966 rolling stock had started to arrive on the line. Buckfastleigh was just as weedy as Ashburton. Notice also that the platform canopy has had to be propped up with two steel columns set in concrete. (Bernard Mills)

The view to the south from Buckfastleigh station was much the same. Note that the signal arms have been removed. This is how the author remembers the site when he first volunteered in June 1966, when this picture was taken. (Bernard Mills)

Work started on restoring the stock straight away and by October three auto coaches had been finished in GWR colours and the weeds had been banished from the track. The temporary support to the platform canopy is still there but the work was being put in hand. (Bernard Mills)

Locos and carriages in the yard at Buckfastleigh in October 1966. 0-6-0 No. 3205 (in front of camera) is in steam, as is 2-6-2T No. 4555 (over to the right). (Bernard Mills)

0-6-0PT No. 6435 stands in front of the loading dock, which has now become temporary storage for loco coal. Carriage restoration work continues, taking advantage of the summer weather in late 1966. (Bernard Mills)

Ex-GWR 0-4-2T No. 1420 in the dock siding at Buckfastleigh being coaled by hand in March 1968. Many of us working on the line thought that the railway would reopen in that year but, due to uncertainties over the future line of the adjacent A38 trunk road, delays in obtaining the Light Railway Order (LRO) from the Ministry of Transport prevented this. No. 1420 was new in November 1933 and after a thirty-one-year working life with the GWR and BR(W) was withdrawn from Gloucester Horton Road depot and was purchased straight out of service by a director of the nascent Dart Valley Railway in November 1964. Fifty years later, No. 1420 is still based on the Ashburton branch. (Bernard Warr)

In the summer of 1968 the Dart Valley Railway was preparing itself for public service. Volunteer efforts intensified, permanent staff were appointed and a series of trial runs from Buckfastleigh to Totnes were undertaken. In this image, we see ex-GWR 0-6-0PT No. 6412 propelling two auto coaches out of Buckfastleigh station on one of these trials (The absence of a 'run-round' loop at Totnes dictated this mode of operation). When the loco was propelling the coaches, as shown here, the fireman was on his own on the footplate and the driver was in a separate driving cab at the front of the leading vehicle. From here he had control of the regulator by means of a control mechanically linked back to the engine and a vacuum brake. Warning of the train's approach was given by use of an externally mounted gong. The system could operate with up to four auto coaches, arranged with two on each side of the loco. (Bernard Warr)

No. 6412 propels its auto train into the lush Devon countryside, bound for Totnes in July 1968. (Bernard Warr)

The first day of public service took place on 5 April 1969 (but only between Buckfastleigh and Totnes, the section to Ashburton now being claimed for the new A38 road subsequently named the Devon Expressway). Auto train working with No. 6412 was employed and the special is seen in this image at Staverton Bridge station, with Brian Cocks conferring with Dave Knowling before they proceeded towards Totnes. Demand was heavy for this historic train and the maximum of four auto coaches (two each side of the engine) were employed. The warning gong on the front of the coach can clearly be seen. (Rex-Conway/BW Collection).

The first steps had already been taken to transform Staverton station from its previously neglected state. The weeds have gone and the signal box has been recovered from a neighbour's garden, where it had been serving as a shed since the railway closed. The train seen heading towards Totnes is a four-coach auto train with No. 6412 providing the power. (Bernard Mills)

As April 1969 proceeded there was no let-up in demand for the train ride and the maximum of four auto coaches were employed regularly. In this view, captured on 27 April 1969, Pannier tank No. 6412 is 'sandwiched' between the four auto coaches on a working from Totnes to Buckfastleigh and is seen near Nappers Crossing. (Bernard Mills)

The terminating point for Totnes trains was something of an anti-climax in the early days of the preservation era – in a cutting with no means of getting on and off! On a quieter day in April 1969, we see 0-6-0PT No. 6435 with two auto coaches approaching the end of its southbound journey. (Bernard Warr)

The Totnes temporary stop board was adjacent to the Branch Up, Outer Home signal and the crew can be seen conferring at this spot before commencing the return journey. In this April 1969 view, there are not too many passengers on board and those that are seem to have their heads out of the windows, seeing why their train has stopped. (Bernard Warr)

With the driver now in the cab of the leading auto coach, No. 6435 begins the return journey to Buckfastleigh. (Bernard Warr)

On the Totnes side of the Stop Board in this early April 1969 view were several rail vehicles. The largest were the two BR Mk 1 carriages with a former engineer's saloon recently delivered from BR and awaiting a tow to Buckfastleigh. In the foreground is a Wickham engineer's personnel carrier and trailer. The large noticeboard proclaims that this is the site of the new Totnes station and the board (and station) awaited erection ahead of the overbridge that can be seen beyond the carriages. (Bernard Warr)

This is the overbridge at Littlehempston (Totnes) that was between the outer and inner branch home signals. In this April 1969 view, work has already begun on providing a run-round loop and the points can be seen directly under the bridge. As later pictures will show, this was not the final position for the loop and it is now some 75 metres to the west. (Bernard Warr)

Littlehempston Bridge again in April 1969 but viewed from the Totnes side. A temporary access from the farm road has been made, some earthworks undertaken and the temporary run-round loop has been roughly laid in. (Bernard Warr)

A final April 1969 view from the same viewpoint as the last image but looking towards Totnes and the West of England main line. Much work remains to be done; note the simple expedient to keep stray vehicles rolling back on to BR territory – tip out two 60-foot rails! (Bernard Warr)

Although the Dart Valley Railway (DVR) was not allowed to operate public services over the section of the line from Buckfastleigh to Ashburton, they were allowed to enter into a short-term lease to use the facilities that it offered. These included the Ashburton station area, which became the locomotive depot and servicing facility. In this image from May 1969, 0-4-2T No. 1420 is preparing to move 'out of steam' locomotives around the yard. In the background can be seen the Ashburton Malthouse. (Bernard Warr)

Driver Brian Cox gets between No. 1420 and 0-6-0PT No. 1369 (one of the Weymouth Dock tanks) to couple them together for a trip to the water column. (Bernard Warr)

The two engines set off for the water column. Note the unrestored 0-6-0PT No. 6430 (between the engineer's saloon and the 12-ton van) and in-service No. 6435 on the left. No. 6430 was purchased by the DVR as a source of spares for Nos 6412 and 6435. (Bernard Warr)

The pair arrive at the water column. Note the very substantial water tank and the extension being built onto the single-road engine shed. (Bernard Warr)

No. 1420 takes water while the driver opens the tool box and prepares to oil round. Note the substantial Ashburton Malthouse chimney. (Bernard Warr)

No. 1369's turn at the water column. Note the substantial brazier for keeping the column frost-free in cold weather. (Bernard Warr)

With two more engines in the consist (Nos 6435 and 1638), the shunting continues. It is believed that the extension to the engine shed was commissioned by the DVR in the belief that they would be allowed to eventually operate a public service through to Ashburton and needed to establish maintenance facilities. Unfortunately, this was not to be and by late 1971 the site was vacated. (Bernard Warr)

Shunting now completed, Nos 1420 and 1369 are back on the Malthouse siding. (Bernard Warr)

This is a shot of Keynsham station near Bristol in May 1970. The town of Keynsham was well known on two accounts: one because it was the home of the Fry's chocolate factory and the second because it regularly featured in advertisements on Radio Luxemburg, but the reader will need to be of a certain age to remember either of these now! The reason for its inclusion here is that the partly dismantled footbridge was purchased by the DVR, originally for use at the new station at Totnes. In the event, it never got as far as Totnes but was put to good use at Buckfastleigh, where it still stands today. (Bernard Warr)

As an employee of the BR Divisional Engineer, the author was able to purchase the timber steps, risers, stringers and handrails as his 'firewood allowance', which cost the princely sum of 5s (£0.25). Long-serving member Roger Gingel can be seen loading this timber onto his lorry ready for the trip to Devon. Just beyond the footbridge was Keynsham station signal box. Unfortunately, its days were numbered as the Bristol MAS scheme, introduced in the winter of 1970, swept away all the manually operated signal boxes in the area. (Bernard Warr)

A concerted fundraising campaign among members of the Dart Valley Railway Association (DVRA) in 1969 and 1970 resulted in the sufficient funds being raised to purchase a 78xx Manor Class locomotive from Woodham's Scrapyard in Barry. The locomotive selected was No. 7827 *Lydham Manor*, a stalwart of the Cambrian Coast Line. The decision was taken to move the engine from Barry to Buckfastleigh by rail and the move took place in June 1970. The following images were captured when the convoy arrived in Bristol for a loco change. (Stuart Warr).

After four years in the scrapyard at Barry, No. 7827 still looks quite presentable (by the standards of BR steam locos at the end of steam operation). The journey from the scrapyard to Buckfastleigh was over 140 miles and at the 15 mph speed limit imposed by BR it was a lengthy business! Here she stands in Bristol West Depot, awaiting a fresh locomotive to continue the journey. (Bernard Warr)

A close scrutiny of the wheel bearings was carried out during the break but all was found to be in order. Grenville Hounsell of the DVRA Bristol Area Group looks on, while Brian Cocks talks to someone off camera. (Bernard Warr)

In due course Warship Class No. 856 *Trojan* arrived to continue the journey. One of the DVR crew attends to coupling up the locomotive. (Bernard Warr)

The convoy sets off on the remainder of its journey to Devon. Most of the restoration work on No. 7827 was carried out at Newton Abbot in the former GWR locomotive works and it returned to steam in 1973. (Bernard Warr)

This view of Buckfastleigh, from the field below Five Lanes Cross, dates from October 1970 and shows the station area and the town before the A38 dual carriageway was built. In the centre of the picture is the valley bottom occupied by both the river and the railway. Several chocolate and cream, GWR-liveried carriages can be seen, as can the station master's house – the white building to the left of the large conifer trees to the left of the carriages. The 1970 version of the A38 road can be seen running parallel with the carriages but slightly higher up and in front of the houses. Contrast this view with the next. (Bernard Mills)

Forty-eight years have elapsed between this 2018 view and the last. Dominating the scene is the A38 dual carriageway, the Devon Expressway, which strides right through the station site. Despite this intrusion, much development of the station area has taken place as the number of industrial-type buildings can testify. Note also the number of new houses that have been built. (Bernard Mills)

By May 1971 the run-round loop at Totnes had been brought into use, freeing the DVR from the shackles of auto train working. This picture taken from Riverford Bridge shows No. 6435 on the front of six carriages heading for Totnes. The coach next to the engine is the Devon Belle observation car. This was originally put into service in 1947 by the Southern Railway on the daily Pullman luxury train of this name running from Waterloo to Ilfracombe and was used on this service until 1954. In use on the Dart Valley, a supplementary fare was charged but there was an on-board bar serving drinks and light refreshments. (Bernard Mills)

The splendid overall roof of Ashburton station enjoyed something of a railway swansong in 1971. The DVR refurbished the buildings, painted the timberwork and replaced all the period signs in the train shed. In this sunny June 1971 view we see 0-4-2 No. 1420 and Small Prairie No. 4555 awaiting their next turn of duty. (Bernard Mills)

One of the stalwarts of the early DVR fleet was ex-GWR Small Prairie 2-6-2T No. 4555. Bought out of service from BR by Patrick Whitehouse and Pat Garland (both of *Railway Roundabout* fame), this was one of the first engines to arrive on the branch. She is seen here approaching Staverton from the Totnes direction in September 1971. (BW Collection)

Ashburton station yard in October 1971. (Bernard Mills)

A view that is lost forever! Taken, in October 1971, from the A38 overbridge at the north end of Buckfastleigh station, looking over the River Dart bridge and into the station yard. It looks so permanent and timeless, yet within a few months all this area was to be obliterated by the embankment that was to carry the new road. (Bernard Mills)

With the construction of the A38 Devon Expressway imminent, the DVR was obliged to quit Ashburton station and the line north of Buckfastleigh. A celebratory day of 'last trains to Ashburton' was organised for 2 October 1971. Apart from the Dart Valley's own train, two special trains were organised to come in from the BR network – one was from Swansea and the other from London (fare for the trip – £3). This image shows newly restored Small Prairie No. 4588 running round the DVR train in Totnes main line station prior to setting off for Ashburton. The author had the privilege of being the guard on this train. (BW Collection)

The DVR special leaving Buckfastleigh, crossing the River Dart and preparing to work hard on the rising grades towards Ashburton. The site of this bridge is now buried beneath the A38 Devon Expressway. (BW Collection)

The first train of the day is seen in Ashburton station yard with 0-6-0PT No. 6435 about to couple up and return the train to Buckfastleigh for stabling. Loco No. 4588, which had brought the train up from Totnes, would remain at Ashburton until needed later in the day. (Bernard Mills)

The next train to come down the line from Totnes was the special from Swansea, which reached its destination in the late morning. The diminutive 0-4-2T No. 1420 was dispatched to Ashburton to return the special to Totnes. In this view the returning Ashburton to Swansea special (1Z80) is about to enter the little used Up platform at Buckfastleigh to allow the special from London Paddington to pass. (Bernard Mills)

On the final approach to Ashburton the twelve-coach special from Paddington passes in the capable hands of Nos 1638 and 6435. As an aside, some enterprising person, keen to get an action shot of the steam train passing, applied grease to the rails, causing a mighty slip. Fortunately, despite the gradient, the engine crews were able to recover the situation and continue to Ashburton. Never one to miss a PR opportunity, Terry Holder, the DVR General Manager, was straight on the phone to the Sunday papers and it did get reported in the following day's editions! (Bernard Mills)

The very last passenger train from Ashburton was the 15.05 Ashburton to Paddington special (1Z45), seen here approaching Buckfastleigh in the charge of Small Prairie 2-6-2T No. 4588. (Bernard Mills)

0-4-2T No. 1420 passes over the car park bridge at Buckfastleigh with a train from Totnes in May 1977. By this time the new A38 was built and a huge embankment had grown across the station goods yard. The signal box was no longer in the right place to control movements and a new one was being built in a more appropriate location. Note the new signal post alongside the train. (Bernard Warr)

Seen in the summer of 1977, this is 0-6-0PT No. 6435, returning to Buckfastleigh from Totnes with six coaches. (Bernard Mills)

Photographed in May 1983, this is the very impressive ex-Great Western signal box on the Up platform at Totnes main line station. From April 1985 Dart Valley services from Buckfastleigh were able to use the Totnes main line station and were controlled by this box on a daily basis. This arrangement lasted until September 1987, when the agreement was terminated by the DVR, citing high costs. The box was closed two months later and control of the line was taken over by the new Exeter signalling centre. (BW Collection)

A special train comprising No. 1420 and the Victorian saloons prepares to depart from Totnes with an evening special to celebrate the centenary of the Permanent Way Institute in July 1984. (Bernard Mills)

Small Prairie 2-6-2T No. 4588 arrives at Buckfastleigh with a special train from the BR network in July 1986. No. 4588 was purchased from Woodham's Scrapyard in Barry in 1971 by the Dart Valley Railway Association for £1,750. The DVR decided it needed the loco quickly and so paid for it to be overhauled by Swindon Works. Upon completion, and despite the total ban on steam traction on the network at that time, it was allowed to return to Buckfastleigh under its own power. (BW Collection).

On a misty April morning in 1989 0-6-0PT No. 1638 follows the course of the River Dart at Riverford as it nears Staverton with a service from Buckfastleigh. (Bernard Warr)

Later the same day, No. 1638 is again seen approaching Staverton, but this time from the Totnes direction. (Bernard Warr)

Arriving at Staverton station. (Bernard Warr)

Warning sign at Staverton. (Bernard Warr)

Conveniently for photographers, the road at Caddaford is alongside the railway line. In April 1989, the track has recently been re-laid with new fencing and a French drain provided. Steaming through the site comes 0-6-0PT No. 1638 with a Totnes to Buckfastleigh service. (Bernard Warr)

In the early morning sunshine of April 1989, No. 1638 (now named *Dartington*) shunts the stock for the first train of the day over the car park underbridge at Buckfastleigh. (Bernard Warr)

Sporting large logo livery, BR Class 50 No. 50045 *Achilles* roars through Totnes on the Up main line with a freight working on 12 June 1989. Built originally to power Anglo-Scottish express trains over the northern fells, the Class 50s were 'cascaded' to the Western Region following the extension of electrification of the West Coast Main Line (WCML) from Weaver Junction (Crewe) to Glasgow in May 1974. The Western Region followed earlier tradition and gave them names after famous Royal Navy ships and used them to displace the ever popular Western and Warship diesel-hydraulic locomotives. The Class 50s themselves were in turn displaced by the coming of the Class 43 High Speed Trains (HSTs) in August 1976 (Paddington to Bristol/South Wales) and May 1980 (Paddington to the West of England). No. 50045 survived for a further eighteen months after this picture was taken, being withdrawn in December 1990. (BW Collection)

On 9 April 1990, the visiting weedkiller train heads in the Up direction past Kilbury Manor and the Buckfastleigh sewage works with Class 20 No. 20904 leading and No. 20901 at the rear. (Bernard Mills)

On a hot summer's day in July 1990, 0-6-0PT No. 6435 simmers in the sun in Buckfastleigh station yard, awaiting the service from Totnes which it will take over. Note the attractive landscaping between the railway and the River Dart. (Bernard Warr)

The former Keynsham station footbridge, now re-erected at Buckfastleigh and providing access from the Riverside Country Park area to the station. The replacement signal box –'Buckfastleigh South Signal Box' – can be seen through the footbridge, with the signalman waiting to receive the single line token from the driver of the approaching Down train from Totnes in July 1990. (Bernard Warr)

The footbridge provides a good vantage point to overlook the whole station. To the right is the Country Park and in the middle are the running and maintenance sheds. The original signal box can still be seen just to the right of the water tower and the once dominant embankment that carries the A38 Devon Expressway has by now (July 1990) disappeared behind strategic tree planting. (Bernard Warr)

With the Dartmoor Hills in the distance, the remainder of the station is shown here in this July 1990 view. The buildings on the Up platform are the typical GWR pagoda-style corrugated-iron store shed: the toilets; the booking office; and the station master's office. The next building along, the former goods shed, houses the museum and a rather cramped carriage and wagon workshop. (Bernard Warr)

The Down train from Totnes arrives and the signalman prepares to collect the single line token from the driver in this timeless July 1990 scene. (Bernard Warr)

A very smart-looking 0-6-0PT No. 1638 prepares to shunt the yard at Buckfastleigh to form up an engineer's train. (Bernard Warr)

Selecting wagons from the yard, the train is formed in Platform 2. (Bernard Warr)

Just one more move to make! (Bernard Warr)

Intending passengers on the Buckfastleigh station platform look on as No. 1638 prepares to leave with the engineer's train in July 1990. (Bernard Warr)

With the 'Toad' brake van added, No. 1638 heads off to the work site on a lovely July 1990 evening. (Bernard Warr)

After the work is completed the Permanent Way gang returns to Buckfastleigh in the brake van. (Bernard Warr)

On 6 September 1991, the 15.20 Buckfastleigh to Totnes service is in the hands of visiting LNER J72 No. 69023. Owned by the North Eastern Locomotive Preservation Group (NELPG), this locomotive can trace its ancestry back to the nineteenth century, when the first examples were built by the North Eastern Railway. Subsequent examples were built by the LNER and British Railways (including this one). (Bernard Mills)

Another visiting engine, this time GWR No. 3440 *City of Truro*, is photographed crossing Nursery Pool Bridge just south of Buckfastleigh, heading for Staverton and Totnes. No. 3440 was reputedly the first steam engine to attain a speed of 100 mph, which it did when running down Wellington Bank (in Somerset) with an 'Ocean Mails' special from Plymouth Millbay to London Paddington on 9 May 1904. (Bernard Mills)

Another picture of *City of Truro*, this time piloting 0-6-0PT No. 7752 (visiting the SDR from Tyseley) round Caddaford Curve with the 10.30 Buckfastleigh to Totnes on 13 June 1992. (Bernard Mills)

Resting in Platform 2 at Buckfastleigh on 23 July 1995 is the 1975-built replica of *Locomotion No. 1* and train. Originally built to take part in the 150th anniversary of the first steam-powered railway, the loco and train are now based at the Beamish Open Air Museum. (Bernard Mills)

J94 Austerity saddle tank *Errol Lonsdale* (carrying the fictitious number 68011) arrives at the developing Totnes Littlehempston station in June 1995. (Bernard Warr)

With the West of England main line in the background, J94 No. 68011 commences running round its train at Totnes Littlehempston station in June 1995. Built in 1953 as No. WD196, this loco spent its working life on the Longmoor Military Railway. In March 1978 it was named after Major General Errol Lonsdale (1913–2003), the distinguished wartime commander and Colonel Commandant of the Royal Corps of Transport from 1969 to 1974. (Bernard Warr)

With Littlehempston bridge in the background, No. 68011 sets out with the 15.00 Totnes to Buckfastleigh service on 14 April 1995. With the closure of the Longmoor Military Railway in 1970, No. 68011 went first to the Kent & East Sussex Railway and then in 1976 to the Mid-Hants Railway. It joined the SDR fleet in 1992 and was sold on again in 2009. After the Second World War the LNER acquired a number of locomotives of this type and classified them as J94. The original '68011' number was carried by one of these until it was scrapped in 1965. (Bernard Mills)

With Staverton Up Distant signal in the background, No. 68011, working the 13.10 Totnes to Buckfastleigh on 14 April 1995, approaches Hood Bridge field. (Bernard Mills)

Arriving at Totnes Littlehempston on 11 February 1996 is No. 7802 *Bradley Manor*, visiting from the Severn Valley Railway. It has worked the 11.00 from Buckfastleigh. (Bernard Mills)

Close to Buckfastleigh and adjacent to the railway is Kilbury Manor. Passing here on 23 March 1996 is visiting 0-4-2T No. 1450, working the 12.45 auto train from Staverton. (Bernard Mills)

Once a resident locomotive on the line in DVR days, No. 1450 visits occasionally and is seen here on a single-coach auto train at Stechford while working the 11.50 Buckfastleigh to Staverton on 30 March 1997. (Bernard Mills)

By the mid-1990s a number of classic preserved buses started to find a home, albeit temporary, on the Buckfastleigh site. Tucked away behind the workshop was this former Devon General, No. 47 (LUO 47F). An AEC Reliance with Willowbrook bodywork, it is seen in 1993. (Bernard Warr)

A view from the Buckfastleigh station footbridge in May 1999, showing how the trees planted on the A38 embankment have now grown enough to hide it from view. Standing in the platform is 0-6-0 No. 3205, which is preparing to depart for Totnes. No. 3205 originally came to Buckfastleigh in working order on 2 October 1965. However, within a couple of years it was whisked away to the Severn Valley Railway and pulled their inaugural train on the opening day in 1970. It remained there for many years before coming south for a spell on the West Somerset Railway and eventually returned to Buckfastleigh in 1998. (Bernard Warr)

Another view of No. 3205 in Buckfastleigh in May 1999. There were originally 120 members of this 2251 class of GWR 0-6-0 locomotives, but No. 3205, which was built in 1946, is the only one to survive into preservation. (Bernard Warr)

An additional loco crew member prepares to join the engine for the first train of the day to Totnes on a dull May morning in 1999. (Bernard Warr)

The fireman looks back down the train as the departure for Totnes takes place. Before coming to the South Devon Railway, No. 3205 suffered a broken crank axle. The repair of such a major component was a challenge but the SDR engineers were able to rise to this and the experience gained was invaluable. (Bernard Warr)

Passing over the car park bridge, No. 3205 makes for Totnes. After a working life of just over eighteen years, half of which were spent at Gloucester, Horton Road (85B), No. 3205 spent its last year and a half in the West Country, being shedded at Exmouth Junction (83D) and finally Templecombe (83G), from where it was withdrawn in June 1965. (Bernard Warr)

Like most heritage railways the SDR has not overlooked the convenience of diesel locomotives. In this picture, former BR Class 25 D7612 rests in the headshunt at Buckfastleigh. New in 1966, it was renumbered 25262 in 1973 and spent the whole of its working life in the Nottingham and Birmingham Divisions. Use on the SDR is mostly for engineering trains and the occasional passenger train when a steam loco is not available. (Bernard Warr)

Driver Dave Knowling confers with the Buckfastleigh signalman in May 1999. Dave was a life-long steam engineman, having started with BR in July 1954 at Plymouth, Laira depot. He volunteered on the infant Dart Valley Railway in 1965 and was taken on to the permanent staff in 1968. He drove the first train in April 1969 and remained employed by the DVR and the South Devon Railway until he retired in 2004. He continued his association with the railway, working as a volunteer one day a week until October 2017. Sadly, he passed away in December 2017. (Bernard Warr)

A view from inside the running shed in May 1999 along the side of 0-4-2T No. 1420, looking towards J94 0-6-0 Austerity No. 68011 *Errol Lonsdale*. (Bernard Warr)

0-4-2T No. 1420, running as No. 1427 on the Milk Train, approaches Bishops Bridge, Staverton, during a photo charter held on 4 March 2000. (Bernard Mills)

Rainwater in Nappers Field provides a perfect reflection for 0-4-2T No. 1420, running as No. 1427 on the Milk Train, as part of a photo charter held on 4 March 2000. (Bernard Mills)

The rainwater pond re-appeared in Nappers Field later in the year as Class 20 D8110 passes with the 15.08 Totnes to Staverton during a diesel gala weekend on 22 October 2000. (Bernard Mills)

Visiting from the Severn Valley Railway is ex-Great Western 0-6-0T No. 813. She is seen here departing Totnes Riverside with the 14.46 goods train to Buckfastleigh on 16 June 2001. No. 813 was originally built for the Port Talbot Railway & Docks Company by Hudswell Clarke of Leeds in 1900 and was absorbed into GWR stock at Grouping in 1922. She was withdrawn by the GWR in 1933 and sold to Backworth Colliery in Northumberland. Nationalisation of the coal industry in 1947 saw No. 813 (now numbered 12 by Backworth) absorbed into NCB stock as their No. 11. Remaining in service until 1967, the loco was purchased for preservation on the SVR, finally returned to steam in 2000. (Bernard Mills)

Having just passed Bishops Bridge signal box, No. 3205 makes her way past the passing loop with the 16.30 Totnes to Buckfastleigh on 10 May 2002. (Bernard Mills)

The developing face of Totnes Littlehempston station, seen in June 2004. The station buildings are impressive and are genuine ex-GWR, having been recovered from Toller Porcorum in Dorset and carefully moved and reconstructed by a dedicated group of volunteers over a number of years. Note the gate across the access to the main line and the Up home signal protecting it. Conveniently passing was a Virgin CrossCountry Class 220 Voyager. The photograph was taken from the Totnes Rare Breeds Farm. (Bernard Warr)

0-4-2T No. 1420 drifts into Totnes Littlehempston station with the morning train from Buckfastleigh in June 2004. Note the signal box under construction. The wooden superstructure was originally Cradley Heath signal box. This was moved in one piece by road to Buckfastleigh, where it was dismantled still further to facilitate a move to Totnes by rail. (Bernard Warr)

No. 1420 prepares to depart from Totnes for Buckfastleigh. Note the unrestored but preserved Class 50 in the bay platform. (Bernard Warr)

Wagon movement instructions on a preserved box van in Totnes bay platform. (Bernard Warr)

Small Prairie No. 5526 starts away from Buckfastleigh with the lunchtime service to Totnes on 2 July 2004. No. 5526 was withdrawn from service by British Railways in 1962 and consigned to Woodham's Scrapyard at Barry in South Wales. She languished there in the corrosive sea air for twenty-three years before being rescued for preservation. (Stuart Warr)

Diesels in waiting. Class 20s Nos 20110 and 20118 await their next turn of duty at Buckfastleigh on 2 July 2004. (Stuart Warr)

Driving Motor Brake Second (DMBS) No. 122100, photographed soon after arrival on the SDR at Buckfastleigh on 2 July 2004. It was the first of its class to be put into service, in May 1958. After working extensively in the West Country, in other parts of the UK and Scotland, it was withdrawn in 1995, and after the removal of asbestos entered preservation. (Stuart Warr)

Ex-British Rail Class 14 D9525 is seen stabled outside the Buckfastleigh PLOG shed (Private Locomotive Owners' Group) on 2 July 2004. (Stuart Warr)

An immaculate Small Prairie, 2-6-2T No. 5526, awaits departure from Buckfastleigh with a train for Totnes in the summer of 2004. (Stuart Warr)

For many years, a bus service around Buckfastleigh was operated on behalf of the SDR. Here, one of the vehicles involved, an ex-Southern National Bedford OB, is seen awaiting passengers in the station yard in June 2005. (Bernard Warr)

In a quiet period between trains, the view from the station footbridge in June 2005 shows how well the tree planting has 'hidden' the A38 Devon Expressway. (Bernard Warr)

Still in June 2005, and looking from the same vantage point, the railway workshops and running shed lie alongside the riverside walk and picnic area. Note the miniature railway track in the roadway to the right of the picture. (Bernard Warr)

Holidaymakers photograph resident 0-4-2T No. 1420 as she departs Buckfastleigh with the lunchtime service to Totnes in June 2005. (Bernard Warr)

The signal man keeps a close eye on the photographer from the 'new' signal box at Buckfastleigh – 'Buckfastleigh South Signal Box' – in June 2005. (Bernard Warr)

Awaiting passengers for the Buckfastleigh circular tour is former Devon General AEC NTT 679, in June 2005. In the station can be seen the GWR super saloon *Duchess of York*, once used by the company on its prestigious express Ocean Liner specials from Milbay Docks in Plymouth to London Paddington. (Bernard Warr)

Partnering the Devon General AEC on the Buckfastleigh circular tour in June 2005 was ex-City of Exeter Corporation Guy Arab IV UFJ 296. (Bernard Warr)

On 1 June 2005, 0-4-2T No. 1420 pauses in the run-round manoeuvre at Buckfastleigh to take on fresh supplies of water. (Bernard Warr)

GWR 0-6-0PT No. 5786 arrives back at Buckfastleigh with the afternoon service from Totnes on 1 June 2005. Note the 'Super Saloon' *Duchess of York* behind the engine. (Bernard Warr)

Back in 1966 the suggestion of a Deltic running alongside the River Dart would have been considered a little fanciful! However, that's just what did happen on 11 June 2005 when No. 55019 *Royal Highland Fusilier* visited the SDR. The loco is seen here alongside the river, skirting the grounds of Dartington Hall with the 14.30 Buckfastleigh to Totnes service. (Bernard Mills)

For the 40th anniversary gala on 5 April 2009, the first train of the day was a goods train from Staverton to Totnes. Running 'light engine' from Buckfastleigh is former Weymouth Dock tank No. 1369, seen passing the River Dart at Caddaford on its way to Staverton to collect the train. (Bernard Warr)

No. 1369 arrives at Totnes Littlehempston station with the goods train from Staverton and passes over the foot crossing that gives access to the Totnes Rare Breeds Farm. (Bernard Warr)

At Totnes a deal of shunting was needed to prepare for the return journey. While this was taking place your photographer took in the details of some of the wagons included in the rake. (Bernard Warr)

An open wagon carefully restored to the livery of a one-time local operator. (Bernard Warr)

It's not often that shunting takes place at Totnes but here we have No. 1369 in the thick of it. (Bernard Warr)

With the train now reformed, No. 1369 sets out on the return journey. Note the ongoing restoration of the Cradley Heath signal box. (Bernard Warr)

With the work done, No. 1369 returns to Buckfastleigh and is seen again at Caddaford. (Bernard Warr)

The second train of the day was the VIP special from Buckfastleigh and this was hauled by 0-6-0PT No. 5786. This locomotive was built by the GWR at Swindon in 1930 and spent all its working life with the GWR and BR(W) in South Wales. In 1958 it was sold to London Transport and became its L92. After eleven years with LT the Worcester Locomotive Society purchased the engine and, after time on the Severn Valley Railway and the Hereford Railway Centre, it brought it to the SDR in 1993. (Bernard Warr)

After running round its train, No. 5786 prepares to return to Buckfastleigh. The plain black livery with the 'cycling lion' emblem carried is typical of the early 1950s. Since preservation the loco has appeared in GWR green and London Transport maroon. The officers' saloon, next to the engine, was for the VIP guests. (Bernard Warr)

To provide a taste of what the first train was like, auto tank No. 6412 was provided to re-enact the opening train with two auto coaches. Looking at the earlier photos in this collection, the reader will note some discrepancies. The coaches of the inaugural train were in GWR chocolate and cream livery rather than the early BR carmine and cream seen here and there were four of them. Even the engine was a 'lookalike'. The real No. 6412 was in such poor condition when acquired from the West Somerset Railway that its major overhaul and return to working order wasn't completed in time for the celebration. What we see here is No. 7752 from the Tyesley fleet, wearing No. 6412's number plates. But, given all these reservations, the SDR was to be congratulated for putting on such a good demonstration and showing new, younger generations what auto train working was all about. (Bernard Warr)

Close-up of No. '6412' arriving at Totnes, showing the floral decoration on the smokebox door. (Bernard Warr)

The celebratory auto train prepares to return to Buckfastleigh with an appropriate headboard on display. The quality of the construction and presentation of the station buildings gives the scene a timeless air. (Bernard Warr)

Later the same day, Small Prairie No. 5542 enters Totnes station from Buckfastleigh. This loco is based on the West Somerset Railway and is owned by the 5542 Fund. (Bernard Warr)

On the Sunday morning, 6 April 2009, Pannier tank No. 5786 takes water at Buckfastleigh prior to working a passenger train. (Bernard Warr)

Pannier tank No. 6435, visiting from the Bodmin & Wenford Railway, arrives at Buckfastleigh with a goods train. Note the fireman with the train staff preparing to hand this over to the waiting signalman. (Bernard Warr)

Former British Rail Class 04 diesel shunter D2246 prepares to do a shunt to release the loco from the recently arrived goods train at Buckfastleigh. Note the very smartly presented Newton Abbot shunter truck. (Bernard Warr)

D2246 propels the goods train into the Buckfastleigh loco yard to allow the train engine to come forward and take water. (Bernard Warr)

Freed of its goods train, No. 6435 is able to come to the water tower and replenish its tanks. (Bernard Warr)

With its tanks now refilled, 0-6-0PT No. 6435 departs with a two-coach shuttle service to Staverton. (Bernard Warr)

0-6-0PT No. 5786 departs Buckfastleigh with the late morning service to Totnes. (Bernard Warr)

Auto-fitted Small Prairie 2-6-2T No. 5526 propels an ECS two-car auto train over the car park bridge and into Buckfastleigh yard. (Bernard Warr)

With the auto train safely out of the way, No. 5786 prepares to leave for Totnes once again. (Bernard Warr)

No. 5526 emerges from the Bishops Bridge Loop and approaches Staverton station with a train for Totnes. (Bernard Warr)

Single-car Class 121 DMU W55000 passes under Riverford Bridge (known locally as Hood Bridge) with the 13.55 Buckfastleigh–Staverton shuttle service on 4 April 2010. Restoration of the early BR green livery had only recently been completed. (Bernard Mills)

Rounding the curve at Hood Bridge Field is ex-GWR heavy freight locomotive No. 3803 with the 15.07 Totnes to Buckfastleigh service on Easter Sunday 4 April 2010. The 28xx GWR heavy freight engines were a very successful design introduced by Churchward in 1903 and continued in production under Collett until they numbered 164. No. 3803 was put into traffic in 1942 and has as its claim to fame the fact that it took part in the 1948 locomotive exchanges, when it was used on the Eastern Region in comparative trials with various LNER designs. It was purchased for preservation in 1984 and after a comprehensive restoration returned to traffic in 2006. (Bernard Mills)

A final image from Easter Sunday 4 April 2010 sees Britannia Class Pacific No. 70013 *Oliver Cromwell* rounding the curve at Hood Bridge Field with the 14.17 Totnes to Buckfastleigh, with No. 5786 out of sight at the rear. (Bernard Mills)

August Bank Holiday Monday fell on 30 August in 2010 and, as a supplement to the regular service, a shuttle service was running between Buckfastleigh and Staverton. The Hood Bridge Permanent Way cabin must have featured in millions of photographs over the years due to the line's proximity to the River Dart. In this picture we see visiting 0-4-2T No. 1450, with a single auto coach, operating the 13.33 Staverton to Buckfastleigh shuttle service. (Bernard Mills)

Another image from August Bank Holiday Monday 2010 sees No. 3205 remembering its days based on the Cambrian lines in Central Wales. Rounding the curve at Hood Bridge Field, No. 3205 is operating the 16.02 Totnes to Buckfastleigh service, despite the headboard that it is proudly carrying. (Bernard Mills)

Near Dartington Hall, three canoeists watch from the river as No. 1450 and a single auto coach steam gently by. No. 1450 and auto No. 178 are operating the 15.45 Staverton–Totnes on Sunday 12 September 2010. This auto coach has genuine GWR parentage, having been constructed by the company in 1930. (Bernard Mills)

On a perfect spring afternoon, Small Prairie No. 5526 has just passed Riverford Bridge and the Hood Bridge Permanent Way cabin while propelling its two auto trailers back to Buckfastleigh. The service is the 15.00 from Totnes on 20 March 2011. (Bernard Mills)

Visiting from the Bluebell Railway on 4 April 2011 is 'Dukedog' No. 9017, seen here near Luscombe Farm. The Dukedogs were a hybrid loco constructed with the chassis from a 'Bulldog' and the boiler from a 'Duke'. At the time of this photograph the loco was only a couple of months away from withdrawal for a major overhaul. (Bernard Mills)

As part of a photo-charter, Class 25 D7612 passes through Stechford with a short milk train running from Buckfastleigh to Staverton on 4 April 2011. (Bernard Mills)

Visiting Dukedog No. 9017 skirts the grounds of Dartington Hall on 8 April 2011 with a milk train heading for Totnes. (Bernard Mills)

On Easter Sunday 24 April 2011, visiting Dukedog No. 9017 steams gently alongside the River Dart near the Dartington Hall Estate with the 17.40 Staverton to Totnes goods train. (Bernard Mills)

Weymouth Dock tank No. 1369 has just passed under Hood Bridge (or Riverford Bridge) and is heading for Buckfastleigh with a short 13.00 service from Totnes on a sunny 11 March 2012. (Bernard Mills)

On a quiet late March day in 2012, 0-6-0 No. 3205 runs round its train in Buckfastleigh station in readiness to work the lunchtime train to Totnes. (Stuart Warr)

Looking a bit sorry for itself, No. 4920 *Dumbleton Hall* stands in the sun awaiting a major overhaul in March 2012. (Stuart Warr)

Detail of *Dumbleton Hall*'s nameplate, seen in March 2012. (Stuart Warr)

Resident Class 25 D7612 is seen awaiting its next call to duty at Buckfastleigh on 29 March 2012. (Stuart Warr)

With a perfect mirror image in the river, Small Prairie No. 5542, sandwiched between auto trailers W228 and W232, skirts the Dartington Hall estate with the 14.45 Buckfastleigh to Totnes on 16 February 2013. (Bernard Mills)

Visiting from the Didcot Railway Centre is the unique GWR steam rail motor No. 93, which is seen passing Kilbury Manor with the 14.00 Buckfastleigh to Totnes service on 17 February 2013. Originally constructed in 1908 at Swindon Works, No. 93 remained as a self-powered carriage until 1934, when the steam motor was removed and the carriage portion converted to an auto trailer numbered 212. It remained in this form until May 1956, when it was used in the Birmingham area as a static office. In 1970 it was purchased by the Great Western Society as a long-term restoration project. This did not start until 1998 and its restoration to a steam rail motor was not completed until 2011, by which time it had become something of a modern-day engineering wonder and a fine example of self-powered coaches in the days before diesel multiple units. (Bernard Mills)

Passing Kilbury Manor with a mixed train is Weymouth Dock tank No. 1369, seen working the 12.17 Totnes to Buckfastleigh on 18 February 2013. (Bernard Mills)

Nicely framed by the overhanging trees and the fast-flowing River Dart at Stechford is No. 1450 and auto trailer W228, working the 11.30 Buckfastleigh to Totnes on 19 February 2013. (Bernard Mills)

A rather work-weary-looking No. 1450 rounds the curve at Caddaford with a single auto trailer (W228) working the 11.30 Buckfastleigh to Totnes train on Tuesday 19 February 2013. (Bernard Mills)

English Electric Type 3 Diesel No. 6737 stands in Platform 2 at Buckfastleigh station on 15 September 2013. New in May 1962, it was originally allocated to Hull Dairycoates shed. It became No. 37037 under the TOPS system in February 1974 and towards the end of its working life was sent to France in August 1999 for use in the construction of the TGV-Méditerranée high-speed rail link. It returned a year later and was put up for disposal in 2003. In January 2004, the Devon Diesel Society acquired the locomotive and brought it to the SDR. (Stuart Warr)

Visiting from the Paignton & Dartmouth Steam Railway is No. 7827 *Lydham Manor*. On a rather rainy 15 September 2013, the crew are refilling the tender tanks prior to working the lunchtime train to Totnes. (Stuart Warr)

Visiting from the Great Central Railway on Good Friday 18 April 2014 is LMS-designed Class 2MT No. 46521. In the image above, it is seen at Stechford while working the 15.02 Totnes to Buckfastleigh service. Although an LMS design, it was built by British Railways at the former GWR Swindon Works in February 1953 and spent most of its working life in Wales. (Bernard Mills)

Another image from Good Friday 2014, this time showing Class 25 D7612 passing Stechford with a short ballast train from Bishops Bridge loop to Buckfastleigh. (Bernard Mills)

Unexpectedly, Buckfastleigh found itself playing host to ex-LNER A4 Pacific No. 60009 *Union of South Africa* from 16 August to 3 September 2015. The loco had failed at Newton Abbot with an overheating bearing while working the Bristol Temple Meads to Par 'Royal Duchy'. The loco was brought through to Buckfastleigh via the Totnes main line connection for repairs to be carried out. The whole operation was time critical as the engine was booked to haul the Borders Railway Re-opening Special with HM the Queen, Prince Phillip and the Scottish First Minister, Nicola Sturgeon, on board. The photograph, from 3 September, shows the engine preparing to leave for the long journey north to Scotland, which involved a detour via Plymouth to turn. Fortunately, all was well and No. 60009 arrived in time to fulfil its role. (Bernard Mills)

During the February half-term holidays, on 16 February 2016, resident 64xx 0-6-0PT No. 6412 passes Staverton Weir with auto trailers W225 and W228 on a sunny winter morning while working the 11.45 Buckfastleigh to Totnes. (Bernard Mills)

Later the same day, No. 6412 is seen passing the 'rapids' at Caddaford with the 14.00 Buckfastleigh to Totnes. (Bernard Mills)

A visitor for the 2017 half-term holidays was ex-London & South Western Railway type M7 0-4-4T No. 30053, which was owned by Drummond Locomotives Ltd and normally resident on the Swanage Railway. It is seen here just outside Buckfastleigh, passing Kilbury Manor with the 13.00 Buckfastleigh to Totnes on 16 February 2017. At the time of the photograph the engine was already 112 years old, having been built in 1905 and been operated by the LSWR, SR and British Railways. After withdrawal in 1964 the locomotive was sold to Steamtown, Bellows Falls, Vermont, three years later, but was repatriated in 1987. (Bernard Mills)

Possibly the oldest locomotive ever to run on the SDR (133 years old at the date of the picture) is Beattie Well Tank No. 30587. It was built in June 1874 for the London & South Western Railway by the Manchester company Beyer, Peacock to a design by Joseph H. Beattie, the LSWR Mechanical Engineer. Most of the class of eighty-five were withdrawn by 1899 but three were retained and transferred to the LSWR Wenford Bridge Line in 1895, where their light axle loading and short wheelbase were ideal for the sharply curved and lightly constructed branch line. Their role was to haul china clay wagons from the dries at Wenford Bridge to the mainline. This became their role until 1962, when they were replaced by Weymouth Dock tanks. Two survived into preservation and No. 30587, by now part of the National Collection, was for many years a static exhibit in the Buckfastleigh Station Museum. However, in 2001 it was taken the Flour Mill Workshops in the Forest of Dean, restored to working order and transported to the Bodmin & Wadebridge Railway for operational use. In this picture it is seen skirting the grounds of Dartington Hall with the 16.25 Totnes to Buckfastleigh service on 16 February 2017. (Bernard Mills)

A night-time picture of No. 30587 in Buckfastleigh Yard on 17 February 2017. Well tanks, once popular with locomotive designers in the mid-nineteenth century, are unusual in more modern times. In a well tank locomotive the water tanks are not mounted above the footplate, but are set low down. On these locomotives there were two tanks, both between the frames: one was above the leading axle, the other beneath the cab footplate. They can just be glimpsed in this photograph. (Bernard Mills)

A cameo scene set up at Buckfastleigh station with professional re-enactors, Pannier tank No. 6412 and appropriate lighting, marketed as 'Branch Line by Night' on 17 February 2017. It could well be a scene anytime from 1955 to 1958, when the line closed to passengers. The author particularly liked the lone lady passenger asking the driver for information while the ticket inspector busies himself with his newspaper! (Bernard Mills)

On a sunny April Sunday afternoon in 2017, resident BR Class 37 No. 6975 runs alongside the River Dart near Dartington Hall with the 15.00 Buckfastleigh to Totnes – a special celebrating railway author Colin Marsden's sixtieth birthday, on 9 April 2017. (Bernard Mills)

Small Prairie 2-6-2T No. 5542 passes Hood Bridge Permanent Way cabin and prepares to pass under Riverford Bridge with the late-running 12.15 Buckfastleigh to Totnes on 22 May 2017. (Bernard Mills)

On the final day of the 2017 Autumn Diesel Gala, the only surviving Class 17 diesel, D8568, eases away from Bishops Bridge with the 14.47 Totnes to Buckfastleigh on 5 November 2017. (Bernard Mills)

Another shot from the last day of the 2017 Autumn Diesel Gala. Resident BR Class 33 D6501 skirts the River Dart near Hood Bridge with Class 37 D6975 at the rear, working the 10.45 Buckfastleigh to Totnes on 5 November 2017. D6501 (new in 1959) is believed to be the oldest surviving BRCW Crompton diesel in existence and has been resident on the SDR since 2005. (Bernard Mills)

Mid-Hants Railway-based LMS Ivatt Class 2 2-6-2T No. 41312 creates an almost perfect mirror image in the River Dart as it passes Dartington Hall estate with the 16.30 Totnes to Buckfastleigh on 7 October 2018. Although built to an LMS design, No. 41312 was constructed by British Railways at Crewe Works and entered traffic in May 1952. Its entire working life was spent on the Southern Region and it was not withdrawn until July 1967, when all Southern steam working ceased. (Bernard Mills)

The First Great Western Laira Depot shunter No. 08483 leads the 13.31 shuttle service from Staverton to Buckfastleigh past Bishops Bridge. On the rear of auto trailer W233 is resident 08 D3721. The date is Friday 2 November 2018 – the first day of the Autumn 2018 Diesel Gala. (Bernard Mills)

Visiting the SDR from the West Somerset Railway to take part in the Autumn Diesel Gala is BR Class 14 D9526. It is seen leaving Bishops Bridge with the 14.00 Totnes to Buckfastleigh service on 2 November 2018. (Bernard Mills)

Recent heavy rain has left a pool of water in Bishops Bridge field, which perfectly reflects former London Transport L92 (ex-GWR 0-6-0PT No. 5786) in the weak winter sunshine. The train is the 14.30 Buckfastleigh to Totnes on Thursday 27 December 2018. (Bernard Mills)

The Train Now Departing... A final image to close this collection shows No. 5542 and two auto coaches at Woodville, heading for Totnes at the end of May 2017. (Bernard Mills)